WORDSONGS-3
Recovery

BY

C. STEVEN BLUE

The Wordsongs Series

Book 3

WORDSONGS-3
Recovery

ISBN 0-9635499-7-9
ISBN13 978-0-9635499-7-6

Editor: C. Steven Blue

Copy Editor:
Katharine Valentino

Proofreaders:
Michele Graf
Adam Levon Brown

Cover & book design by C. Steven Blue

Published by:

ARROWCLOUD
PRESS

For more information go to www.wordsongs.com

Album Contents:

Dedication...

This book is dedicated to all who are struggling
to recover from the pain life throws our way,
whether it be from abuse, addiction, grief or illness.

For all of those suffering the pain of life's hardships,
I dedicate this book to you. I hope it brings you comfort.

...Quotation...

Your pain is the breaking of the shell
that encloses your understanding.
Even as the stone of the fruit must break,
that its heart may stand in the sun,
so must you know pain.

*Khalil Gibran

*From *The Prophet*, copyright © 1923, by Khalil Gibran

...Introduction...

WORDSONGS–3, Recovery is the third album in The Wordsongs Series. The pains of life do not spare any of us. We all struggle and look for something to ease the pain. This book follows the broken dreams of a lonely man who used drugs and alcohol to cope with the pain in his life. Observe his broken dreams and struggles on side one and his re-awakening to a new life in recovery on side two. In this inspirational and innovative book, C. Steven Blue presents another great set of heartfelt wordsongs.

The Wordsongs Series

Each book in this series contains 20 pieces designed to be similar in scope to a music record album, with side one and side two, but instead of songs it is made up of a style of poems called wordsongs. Each book is a concept album, with a general theme running through it, told in verse format.

Wordsongs are the original creation of C. Steven Blue, who also created a definition for this concept:

word'song, n. [AS. wordsong.]
   1. a poem that is like a song or could be a song
   2. verses that tell a story in song-like rhythm, often with a refrain
   3. a song that you read

*Note: The wordsongs in this book are extracted from the 186 page, full-length book by C. Steven Blue: S.O.S. ~ Songs Of Sobriety ~ A Personal Journey Of Recovery. That book took over 20 years to write and covers the first 10 years in the recovery process. More information on that book can be found here, www.wordsongs.com/sos

...Inspiration

. . . If music speaks, do words sing?

Some music speaks to your senses without words.
Wordsongs sing to your senses without music.
Wordsongs speak to your inner rhythms.

The 20 wordsongs in this album tell a story.
Any music that they sing to you . . .
must come from the inner ear of your own imagination;
the musical tapestry of your mind.

Turn the pages and listen . . .
to these words.

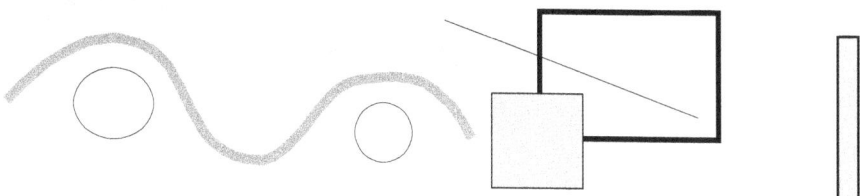

Side One . . .

1

Chair Dreams

Sitting in my chair
Staring out my window
Dreaming about all the things
I'm gonna do . . . and see . . . and be

You're gonna love me
And it's going to be the best love ever
If I can just get out of this chair
And get it together

Chair dreams
Take me here and there
Chair dreams
Take me everywhere

Chair dreams
Seem so crystal clear
        For a moment
But then they're gone . . . again

And it's just another chair dream

I know I was gonna have
        A hit song
And a house in the country
Sit in a rocker on my front porch
With endless inspiration
I know I was gonna paint
        My masterpiece
And write a prize-winning novel

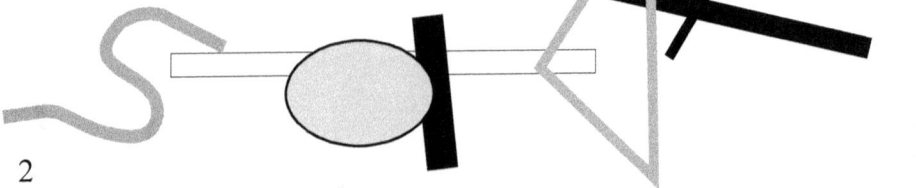

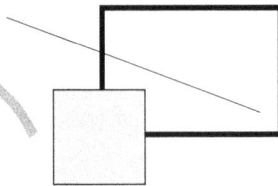

And I remember it sometimes
When I'm high enough

But I just can't seem
To get out of this chair
Can't seem to get motivated
To go anywhere

And my dream slips away
To the back of my mind
Till another day
When the right combination finds . . .
My chair dreams

Chair dreams
Take me here and there
Chair dreams
Take me everywhere

Chair dreams
Seem so crystal clear
        For a moment
But then they're gone . . . again

It's just another chair dream

Sitting in my chair
Staring out the window
Dreaming about all the things
        I'm gonna be

You're gonna love me
And it's going to be the best love ever
If I can just get out of this chair
And get it together

Yes . . . chair dreams
Take me here and there
My chair dreams . . .
They take me everywhere

Chair dreams
Seem so crystal clear
        For a moment
But then they're gone . . . again

It's just another chair dream

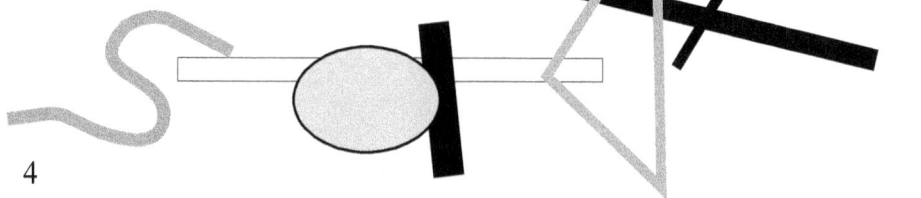

Chair dreams
Take me here and there
Chair dreams
Take me everywhere

Chair dreams
    —Take me outta here

Chair dreams
Seem so crystal clear
        For a moment
But then I'm . . . gone again

It's just another chair dream

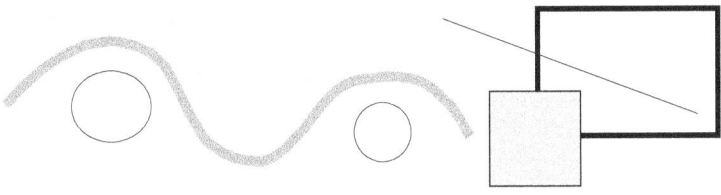

Barroom Blues

Standing here
at the edge of the bar,
wine glass in my hand.
My eyes are red
and you can see their sadness,
but I just don't understand.

Why won't you come over
and talk to me?
I want to be a part of you.
You all seem so happy,
          but I . . .
I just don't know what to do.

I've got these silent, withdrawn,
barroom blues
          again.
Don't know how
I can go on anymore.
I think it's the end.

Yeah, I've got these silent, withdrawn,
barroom blues
          once again.
And no matter what happens,
it seems . . .
like I just can't win.

Why am I here alone
at the end of the bar?
Think I'll have another shot!
Then maybe you'll think
I'm good enough,
'cause I sure want what you've got.

Why can't I
just quit this drinkin'
and get on with my life?
Where is mine—where is she
and why is everything
so screwed up in my life?

I've got these silent, withdrawn,
barroom blues
        again.
Don't know how
I can go on anymore.
I think it's the end.

Yes, I've got these silent, withdrawn
barroom blues
        once again.
And no matter what happens,
it seems . . .
like I just can't win.

—No, I just can't win!

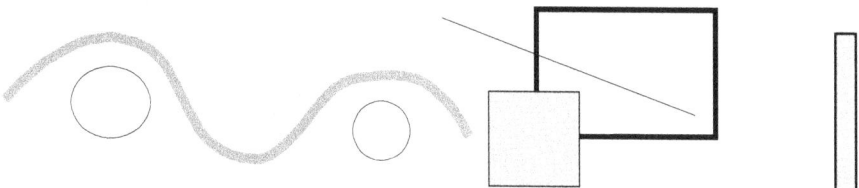

I'm so messed up!
I've been here
so many times before.
Think I'll just, uh . . . drink
till I black out in the back of my car.
Then nothing will matter
or hurt . . . anymore!

> Barroom blues!
> No, I just can't win.

Brighter Day

Why do I feel
So full of love
Yet no one seems
To want it

I have so much
Inside to give
Why won't someone
Take it

Oh I hunger
For that brighter day
When I wake up
Beside you

To hear you say
You'll stay
I've been waiting so long
For that brighter day

I'm not afraid
To love
Though I've had my share
Of being let down

But where's the one
Who shares my faith
The one who's not scared
To stick around

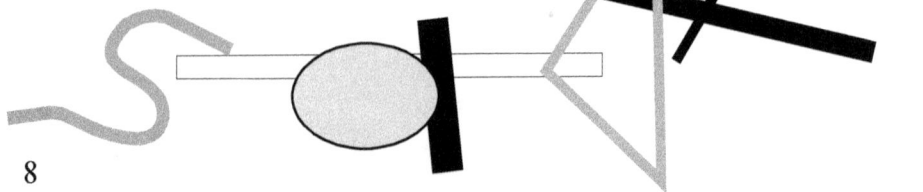

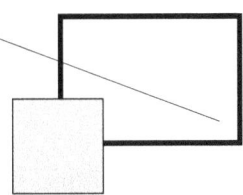

I know it's been said
In better ways
But don't you know
I need you

Yet every time
I feel I'm close
Seems I can't get anywhere
Near you

Why do I feel
So full of love
Yet no one seems
To want it

I have so much
Inside to give
Why won't someone
Take it

Oh, I hunger
For that brighter day
When I wake up
Beside you

To hear you say
You'll stay . . .
I've been waiting so long
For that brighter day

9

Oh, How You Guide Me

In the fellowship around me,
it never ceases to astound me
how your message comes across
        loud and clear,
and all I have to do to find it
        is stay here;

to be reminded day by day,
there is a way for those like me
        to go.

And I know,
or I've made a decision
and come to believe . . .

Oh, how you guide me.
Thank you for staying beside me.
The need to hide is leaving
        day by day.
I'm finding a way
        to live
in the gifts you give.

Sometimes,
when I think I'm losing
        it all,
you show me I am winning.
I see it come full circle
        once again.

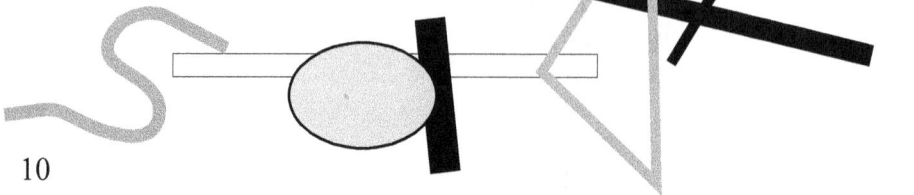

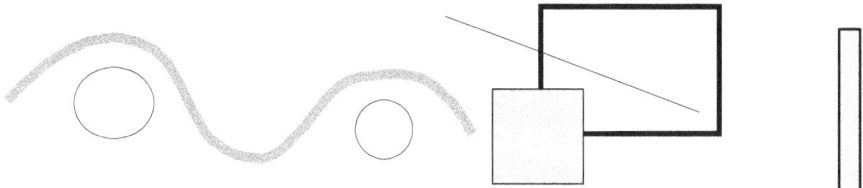

What more can I say,
but to thank you each day,
for showing me the way
      to go.

And I know,
or I've made a decision
and come to believe . . .

Oh, how you guide me.
Thank you for staying beside me.
The need to hide is leaving
      day by day.
I'm finding a way
      to live
in the gifts you give.

Oh, how you guide me.
Thank you for staying beside me.
The need to hide is leaving
      day by day.
I'm finding a way
      to live
in the *freedom* you give.

Thank You, H.P.

I just want to thank you
For giving my life a lift
For the peace that's inside
And the light that I see

Thank you, Higher Power
For giving me my gift
Thank you, H.P.
For that feeling in me

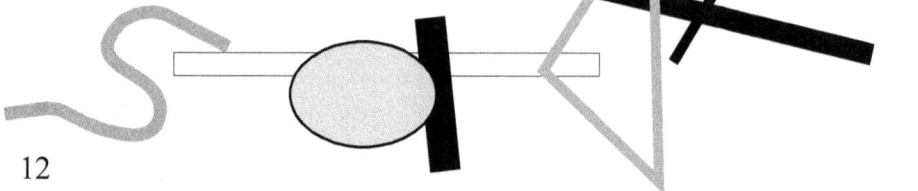

I ask you each morning
Because it's not finished yet
And I thank you each night
So I'll never forget

You keep the strength up inside me
When things all seem wrong
With you here beside me
I know I belong

And I just want to thank you
For giving my life a lift
For the love that's inside
And the light that I see

Thank you, Higher Power
For giving me my gift
Thank you, H.P.
For that feeling in me

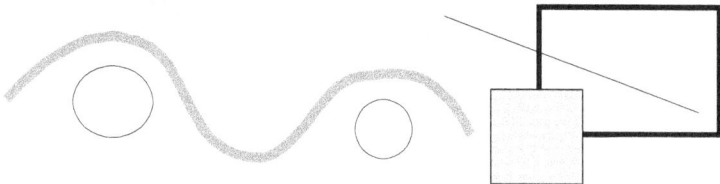

When I'm angry . . . confused . . . or just hurt
You are there
And the strength that you give
Helps me get up and share

When I think I am lost
You show me I'm found
When I think there is no one
You're always around

I just want to thank you
For giving my life a lift
For the peace that's inside
And the light that I see

Thank you, Higher Power
For giving me my gift
Thank you, H.P.
For that feeling in me

Three Forty Four

It's three forty four
and the dealer's knockin' at my door.
Go away—please, now,
and set my mind at ease.

I've felt that pain many times before.
I don't want to feel it anymore,
so go away—please, dealer,
leave me alone.

Lord help me!
Don't let me answer!
I'm so vulnerable
right now.

I want to shut out
the pain inside,
and the dealer knows
just how.

Please, oh God,
make the knockin' go away.
I like the way I feel life now;
it's getting better day by day.

I feel so alone right now.
Stay by my side.
That old pain came back today.
I broke down and cried.

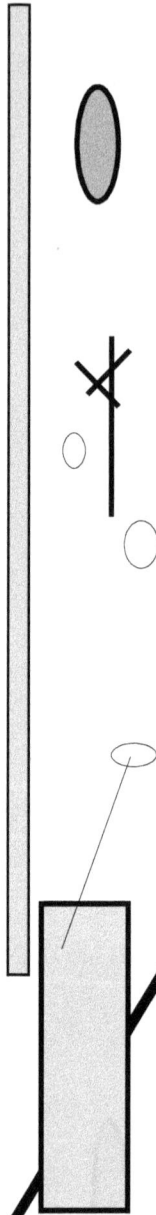

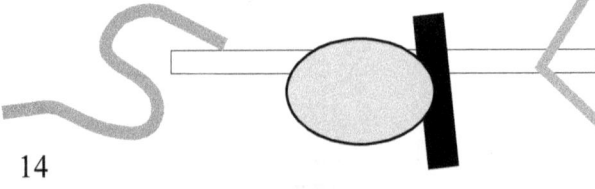

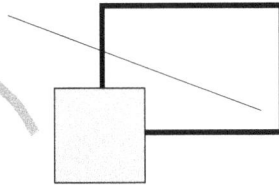

Tears welled up in me.
Resentments were felt.
But it's still not as bad
as when the dealer dealt.

So help me walk through
this pain once more,
so I won't have to wake up
with my face on the floor.

It's three forty four
and the dealer's knockin' at my door.
Go away—please,
and set my mind at ease.

I don't want to score!
I don't want to be sore!
I don't want you no more—for sure!
And it's three forty four.

Turn It Over

When you're down
And the world seems wrong
When you feel
Like you don't belong

When it seems
That there's no way out
And you need to know
What it's all about

Turn it over
To someone who understands
Turn it over
To the one who guides your hands

Turn it over
With a little shove
Turn it over to love

When it's all gone
And you don't know why
And you need someone
But you want to cry

And you want to reach out
But you just can't try
So all you can think is
You want to die

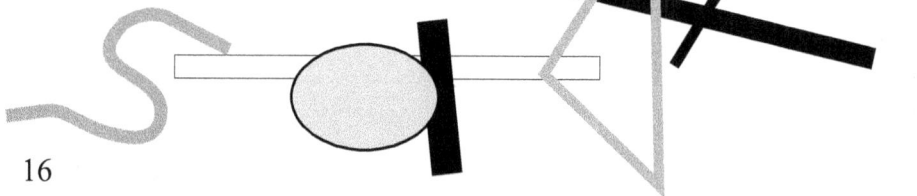

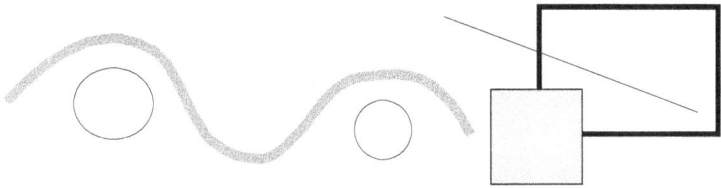

Turn it over
To someone who understands
Turn it over
To the one who guides your hands

Turn it over
With a little shove
Turn it over to love

When you're alone
No one seems to care
You want to know
Is there anybody out there?

'Cause it seems
That no one is like you
And you just don't know
What there is you can do

Turn it over
To someone who understands
Turn it over
To the one who guides your hands

Turn it over
With a little shove
Turn it over to love

When it's so confusing
And you want to rearrange it
But you know inside
You just can't change it

17

And you feel your back
Is up against the wall
And the ladder you've climbed
Is a long way to fall

Turn it over
To someone who understands
Turn it over
To the one who guides your hands

Turn it over
Here's a little shove
Turn it over to love

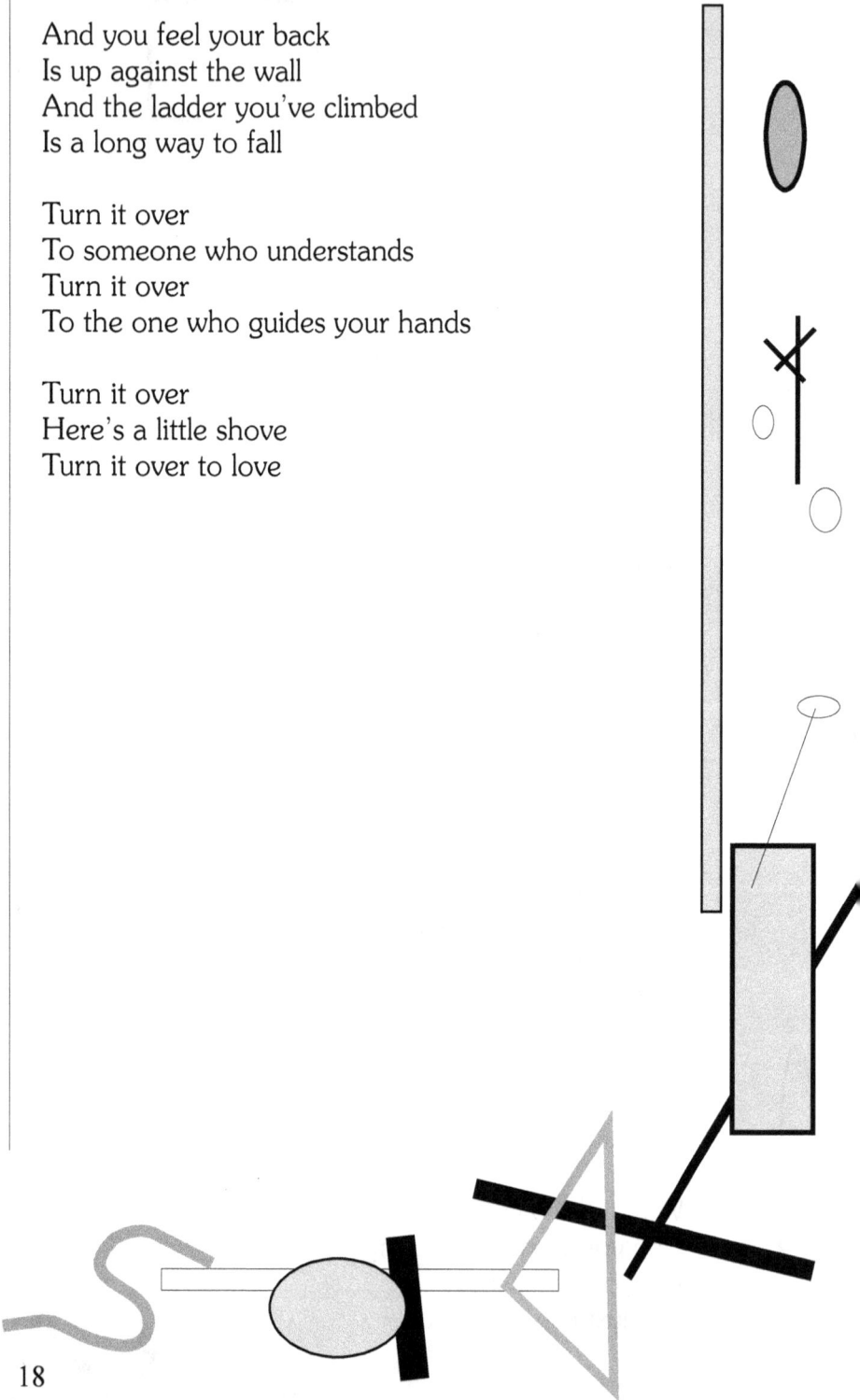

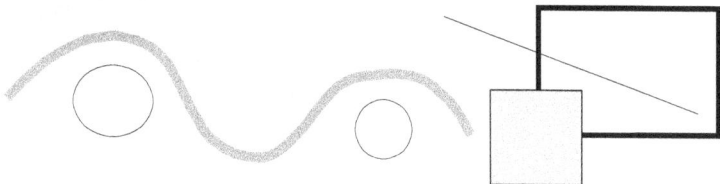

Your Troubled Mind

wake up
     wake up
your inner self

take it off the shelf
and live

make up
     make up
your troubled mind

there is so much
you have to give

aspire to yourself
for change

because
it's an inside job

don't let obstacles
set you back

your inner power
will guide you along

19

get healthy
by following your dreams

get strong
by knowing you belong

and how do you know?
        by growing

take a risk
and persevere

wake up
        wake up
your inner self

take it off the shelf
and live

make up
        make up
your troubled mind

there is so much
you have to give

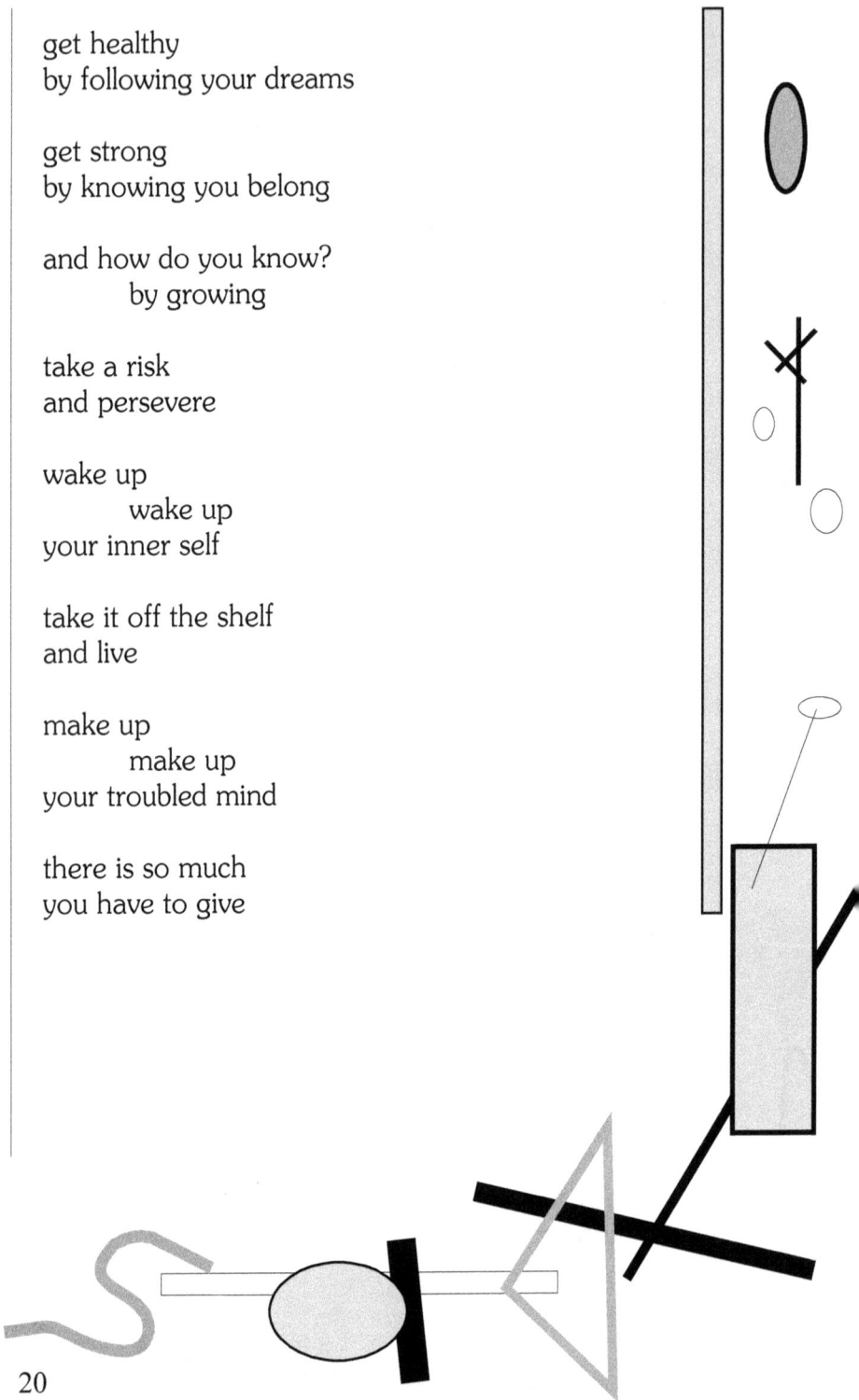

Brand New Day

You wait for her to come
But she can't wait to go
You want to help her make it
But she wants to steal the show

Your head is pounding
Your legs ache too
Can't stand the feeling
That she doesn't need you

Don't it make you wanna run
Don't it make you wanna sail away
Don't it make you hunger
For a brand new day

Your heart starts thumping
When she calls you again
You pace the floor, watch the door
To let her in

It's then that you remember
She may not come around
It seems that when you need her
She never can be found

You're bound again to wonder why
Like so many other days
Deep inside you feel like cryin'
Don't it make you crazy

Don't it make you wanna run
Don't it make you wanna sail away
Don't it make you hunger
For a brand new day

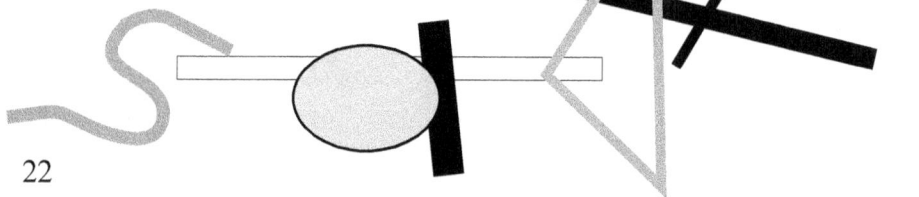

And though you can't figure out
What all the pain is for
The waves break on the shore once more
And morning's at your door

You've got to let her go now
Take care of yourself
Got to take your love for her
And put it on a shelf

'Cause who is gonna fill your heart
Who's gonna take care of you
No one is gonna really love you
Unless you do

Don't it make you wanna run
Don't it make you wanna sail away
Don't it make you hunger
For a brand new day

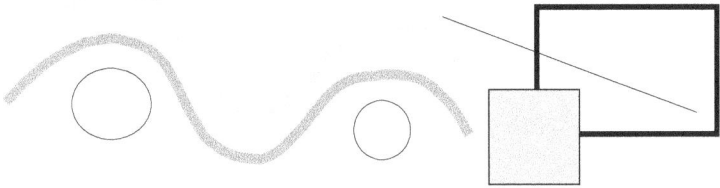

When it's over
And you're all alone
You've got to get up
And carry on

Take a stand where you are
Start to live like you mean it
Pretend you see the sun shine
Until you see it

The New Frontier

Here I sit
in my wayward cubicle;
larger than some,
life just begun.

And I'm grateful for
the chance to be here;
on the verge
of a new frontier.

To go forth by choice,
not feel stuck behind walls.
The present, the future,
my destiny calls.

And I'm listening finally,
isn't it strange?
  Intuition
brings trust for the change.

While the faith that I've gathered,
in just a short time,
gives me strength as I watch
my whole life start to rhyme.

I'm excited by the prospect
of new frontiers,
after so many wasted
and lonely years.

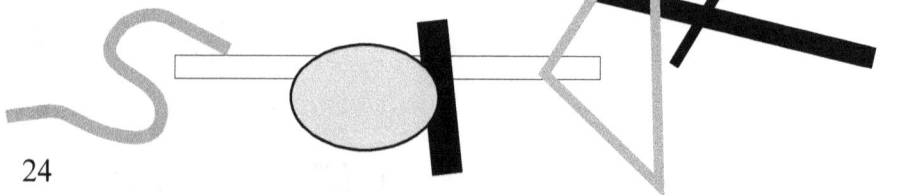

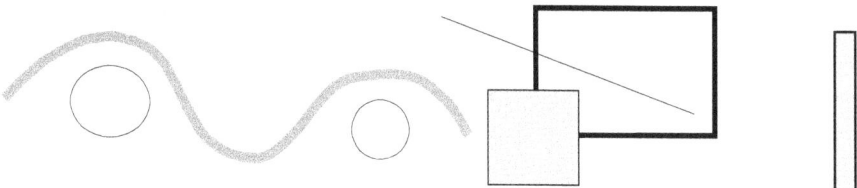

But they weren't really wasted.
I have no regrets
because what one wants
one usually gets . . .

And it took all of that
to get me right here.
All I can say is
I know this quite clear:

After so many wasted,
lonely years,
I'm heading into
new frontiers.

I'm ever so grateful
for the chance that is here.
I'm heading into
the new frontier.

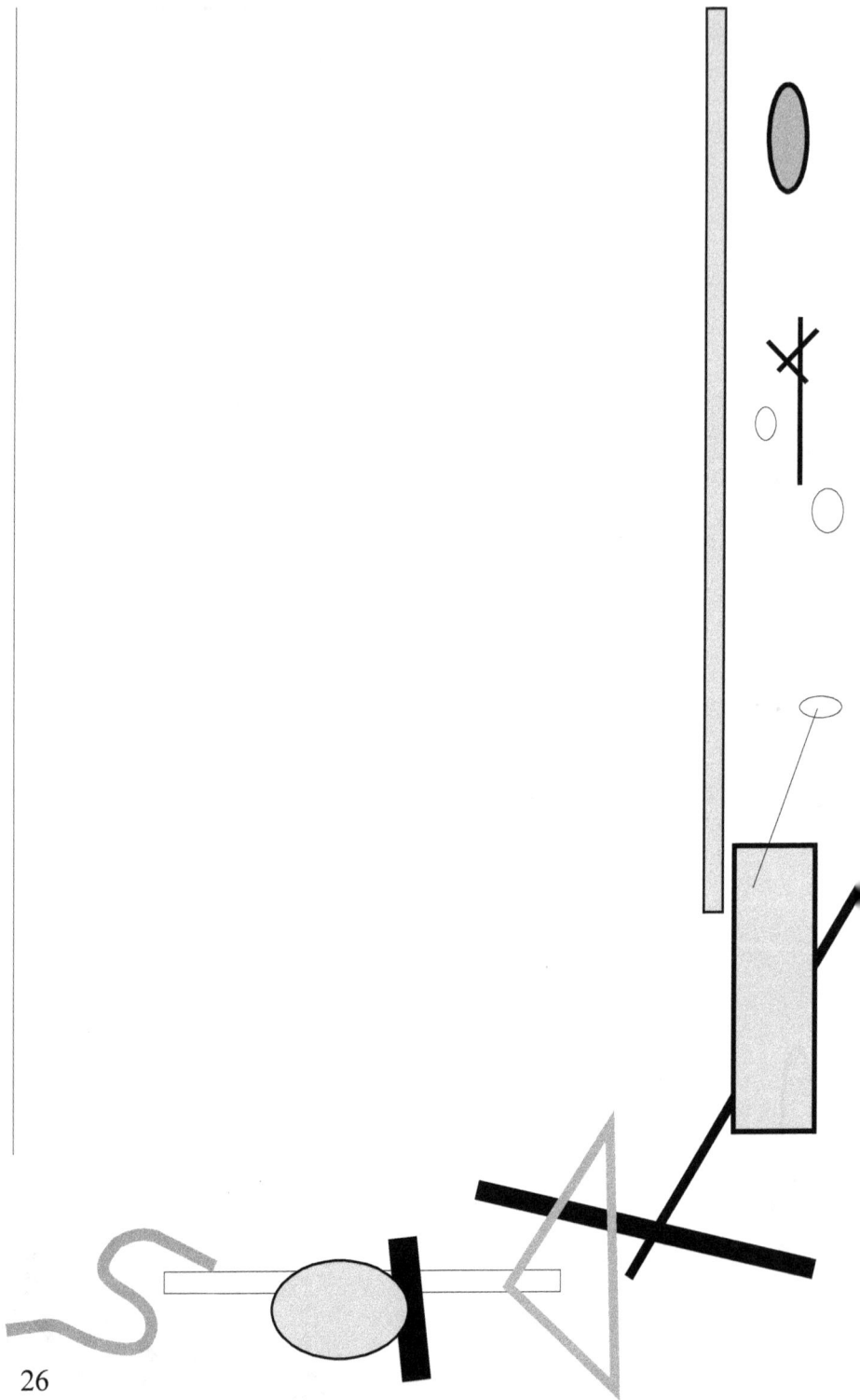

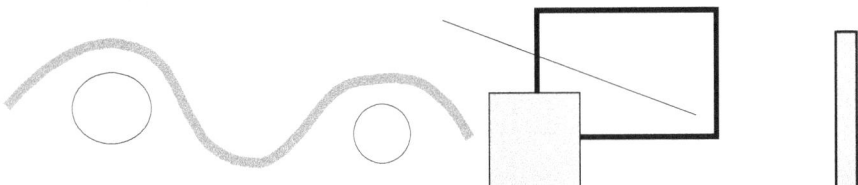

Side Two . . .

27

Collective Individualism:
Once In A Blue Moon

Once in a blue moon
Comes a reason
Come on . . . join in
It won't be treason
The poison in your life
      Be gone!
Carry on
In collective individualism

Once in a blue moon
You can tell
Choose . . . to return
From a living hell
Now is the moment
      To be strong
Carry on
In collective individualism

A wave washes over me
Where the hell have I been
I feel . . . and now I see
It's time to cash
My resentment chips in
It's time my ship came in
It's time to live again

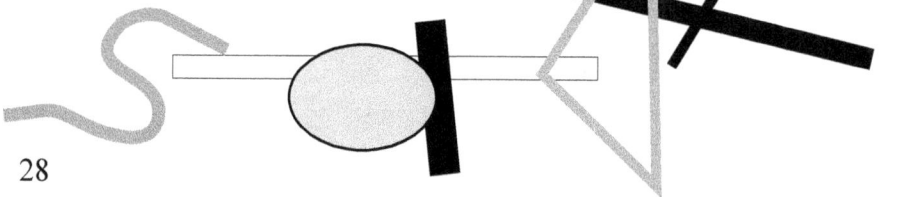

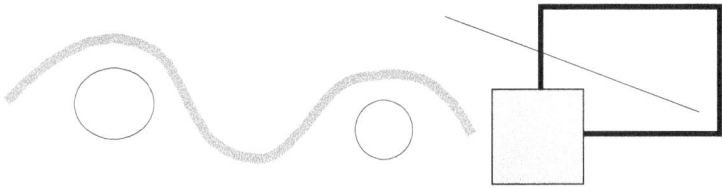

Once in a blue moon
Hear the call
How . . . in heaven
Did I fall
Now is the time
        To belong
Carry on
In collective individualism

Feeling sucked in
By the current
Surrender . . . to be free
Rise up to yourself again
        Naturally

Once in a blue moon
Come what may
You . . . can recover
Day by day
Dreams do come true
It won't be long
Just remember to be strong
        And carry on
In collective individualism

Surrender To Win

I guess I tried
To control you
Have you do it my way
Thought I knew so much better
How to show you

I always hoped
You'd have someone
Of your own
To make you smile

How was I to know
I had to let you go
To set *me* free

Letting go
Letting go
It's the only answer
Don't you know

I had to surrender
To win
So I could begin again

I wanted so hard
To show you
That life could be okay
But I didn't know quite
How to tell you

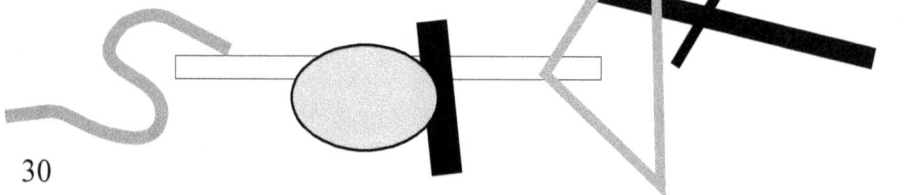

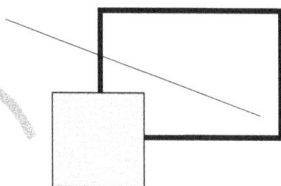

I never thought
You'd find someone
Of your own
To see you smile

How was I to know
I had to let you go
To set you free

Letting go
Letting go
It was the only answer
I didn't know

I had to surrender
To win
So I could begin again

It's easier now
To let it go
Let life have its own way
Now I know much better
How to surrender

And now . . .
You have someone
Of your own
And I watch you smile

How was I to know
I had to let you go
To set *us* free

Letting go
Letting go
It's the only answer
Don't you know

I had to surrender
To win
So I could begin again

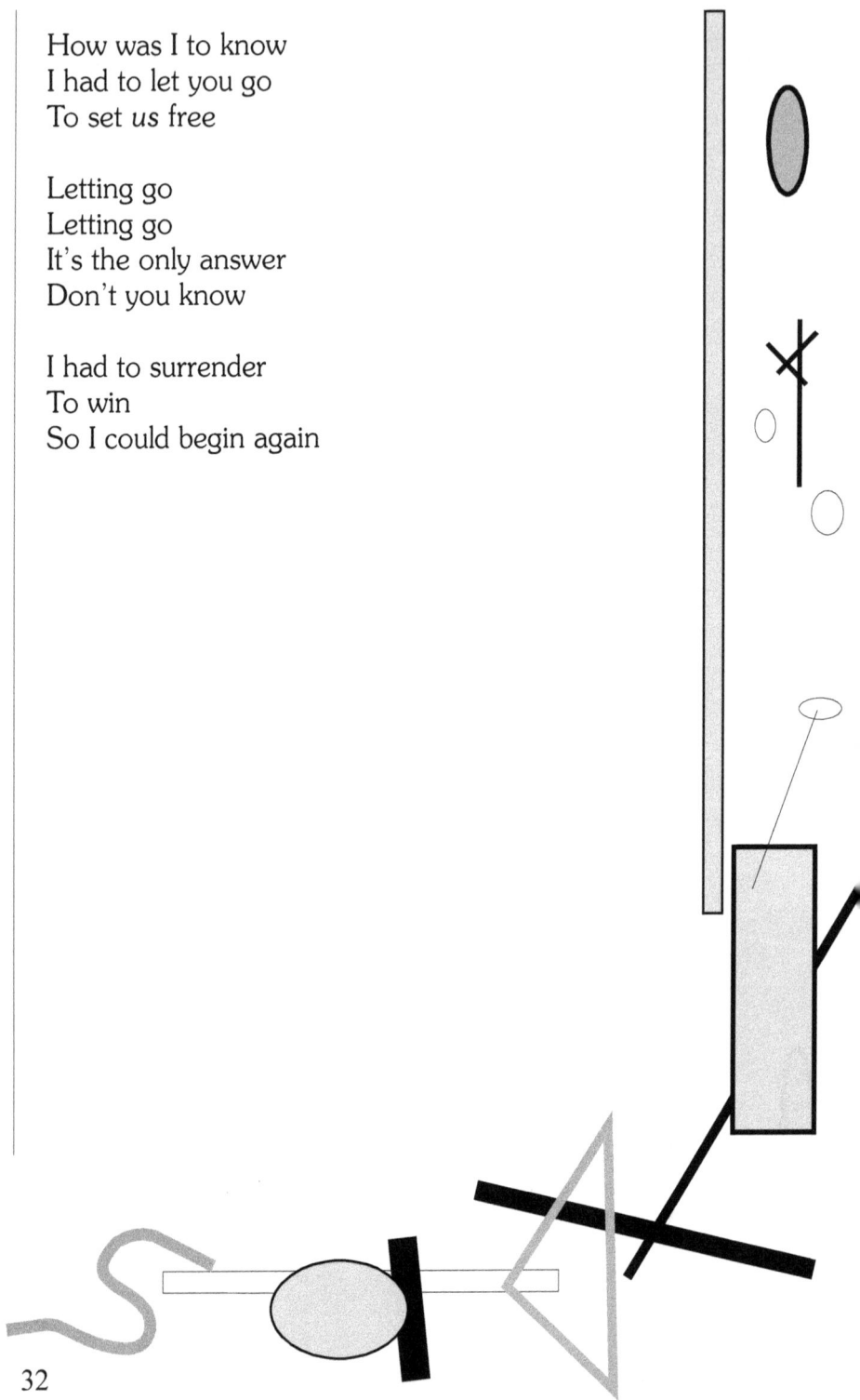

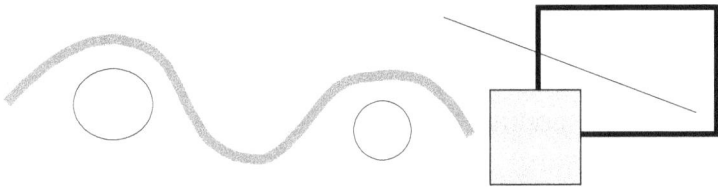

Lucky Ones

I did what I could
And I did what I should
And sometimes I did . . .
What I should not do

I always did my part
Tried to stay true to my heart
Even though I hurt the ones
I loved . . . like you

I'm one of the lucky ones
I've lived long enough to tell you
      I'm alive!
I'm one of the lucky ones
I did what I had to do
      To survive

I'm one of the lucky ones
I got through it still intact
I'm one of the lucky ones
And I'm never looking back

Now it's very hard work
To try and stand up straight and tall
It takes a strong foundation
To know that you won't fall

And if you work it with courage
You can be alive too
So don't you get discouraged
It will be there for you

I'm one of the lucky ones
I've lived long enough to tell you
　　　　I'm alive!
I'm one of the lucky ones
I did what I had to do
　　　　To survive

I'm one of the lucky ones
I got through it still intact
I'm one of the lucky ones
And I'm never going back

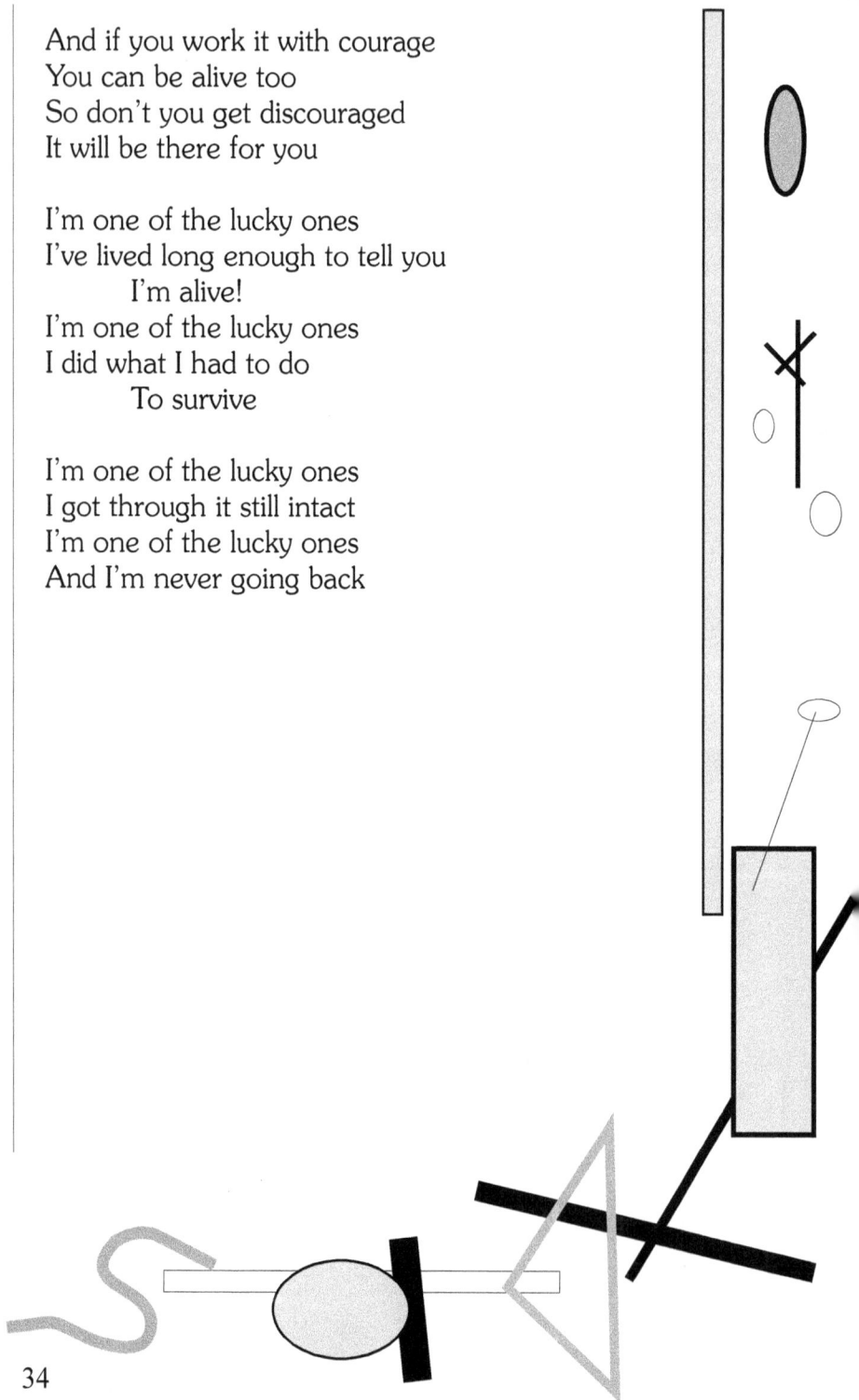

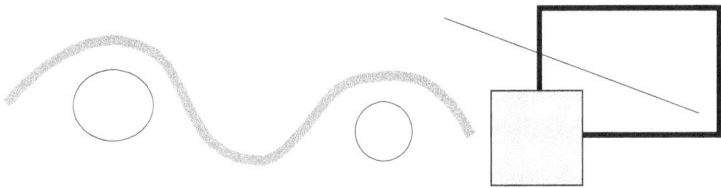

Dawn Is Rising

Having been given
the free will to choose,
you now have a path of your own.
You may choose to follow,
or you may go it alone.

Having been given
a brand new voice,
you now have a song to sing.
You may choose to ignore it
or share the joy it can bring.

Dawn is the song of today.
Sing it to me now.
Dawn—the song of tomorrow.
Far gone . . . the long time sorrow.

Dawn is rising
all around me.
In the here and now
It has found me.

Dawn is rising
on a brand new day.
Never knew it could happen
this way.

35

Having awakened
to a brand new foundation,
how quickly you have grown,
though it may take a little bit longer
to claim it as your own.

Having now
the knowledge and beauty
of joy and grace in your life,
you can reclaim
your new-found freedom
without so much fear of the strife.

Dawn is the song of today.
Sing it to me now.
Dawn—the song of tomorrow.
Far gone . . . the long time sorrow.

Dawn is rising
all around me.
In the here and now
It has found me.

Dawn is rising
on a brand new day.
Never knew it would happen
this way.

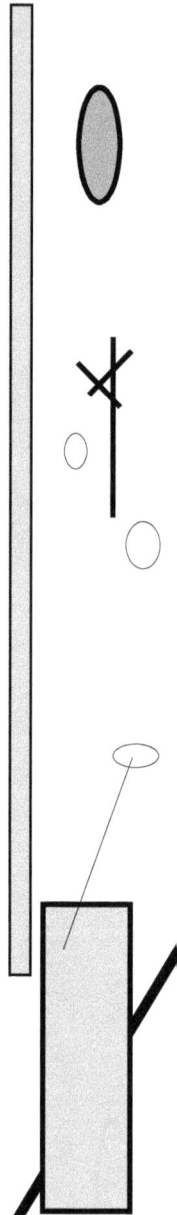

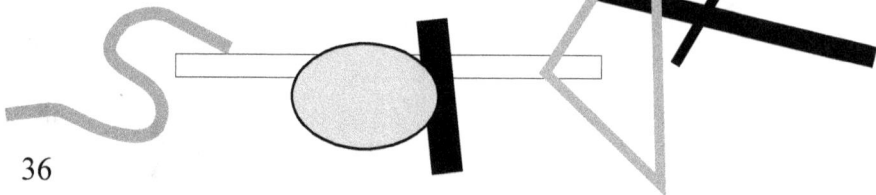

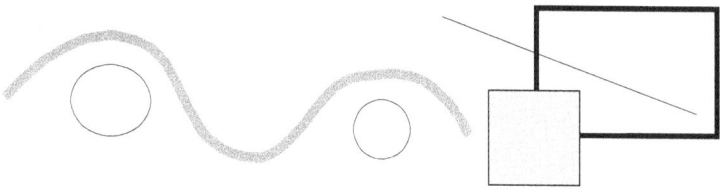

Rest In Peace

Why is it so easy
To solve other people's problems
Yet so hard to solve your own
Take a stand . . . NOW
Live your dreams
Then see how much you've grown

Don't you know . . .
Everyone in the world
Has got their own life to live
So save yourself first
Just don't stomp on others
To do it

It's hard to live
It's a mighty hard life
It's hard to give
When there's so much strife

But when it's all over
You are left with you
So do what you can live with
And leave the rest in peace

You want to help everyone
But neglect your own needs
You want to do what's right
But fail to see people's greed

37

Don't you know . . .
Everyone in the world
Has got their own karma to bear
So save yourself first
Just remember to show others
You care

It's hard to live
It's a mighty hard life
It's hard to give
When there's so much strife

But when it's all over
It's you . . .
That you are left with
So do what you can live with
And leave the
Rest in peace

It's hard to live
It's a mighty hard life
It's hard to give
When there's so much strife

But when it's all over
It's you . . .
That you are left with
So do what you can live with
And leave the . . .
R.I.P.

The Edge Of Things

Here I sit . . .
On the edge of things
Afraid to walk near the Sun
Thrown by the great hand of Destiny
Yearning for dreams yet begun

Out from the sky
Comes the blue light of Love
Shining like all that could be
Strikes me awake
For the first time in ages
Reminds me of what I can see

Reminds me I sing
For the ones still in cages
Convey bits and pieces
That come out in stages

And play to an audience
Fraught with despair
To shine some hope down
Through the darkness they share

I'm sitting here . . . perched
On the edge of things
You wait for me to recite
Born from the image
Of feelings I've known
Or gathered from dreams in the night

You gaze in my eyes
With the sadness of tears
For the Lovers of Love
Who still fall . . .
While I sing you the tales
Of the true ones in time
Who . . . knowing their fate
Still risk all

Reminds me I sing
For the ones still in cages
Convey bits and pieces
That come out in stages

And play to an audience
Fraught with despair
To shine some hope down
Through the darkness they share

Here I sit . . .
On the edge of things
Daring to walk near the Sun
Thrown by the great hand of Destiny
Loving the dreams I've begun

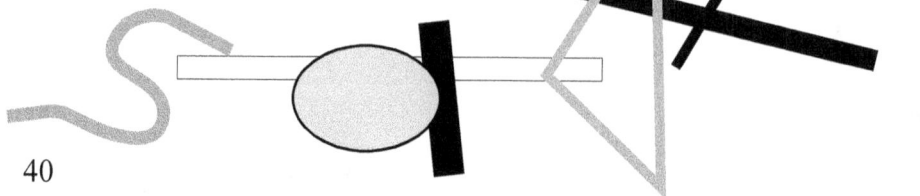

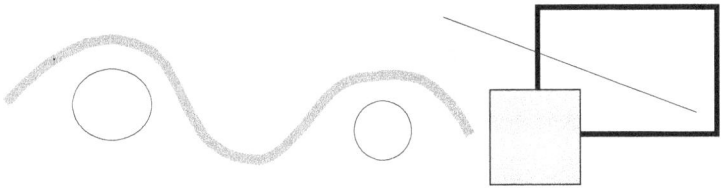

Simply Satisfied

Gratefulness comes soon and quick
These days it seems
And I am full of gratitude
For the scope of my dreams

I am easily satisfied
It's not too much
It's so much
And I am simply satisfied
By your touch . . .
Your touch

I don't care what they say
Or what they think about me
For reality came back today
And paid a call, you see

And I was here to participate
In the simple act of being
In the time and place
For the simple act of seeing

That I am easily satisfied
It's not too much
It's so much
And I am simply satisfied
By your touch . . .
Your touch

41

Every day I'm grateful now
Just to be alive
For I am living on borrowed time
It's a grace to survive

And if I'm here tomorrow
It's only because of you
Now I can see with clearer eyes
The sun shine through

And I am easily satisfied
It's not too much
It's so much
And I am simply satisfied
By your touch . . .
Your touch

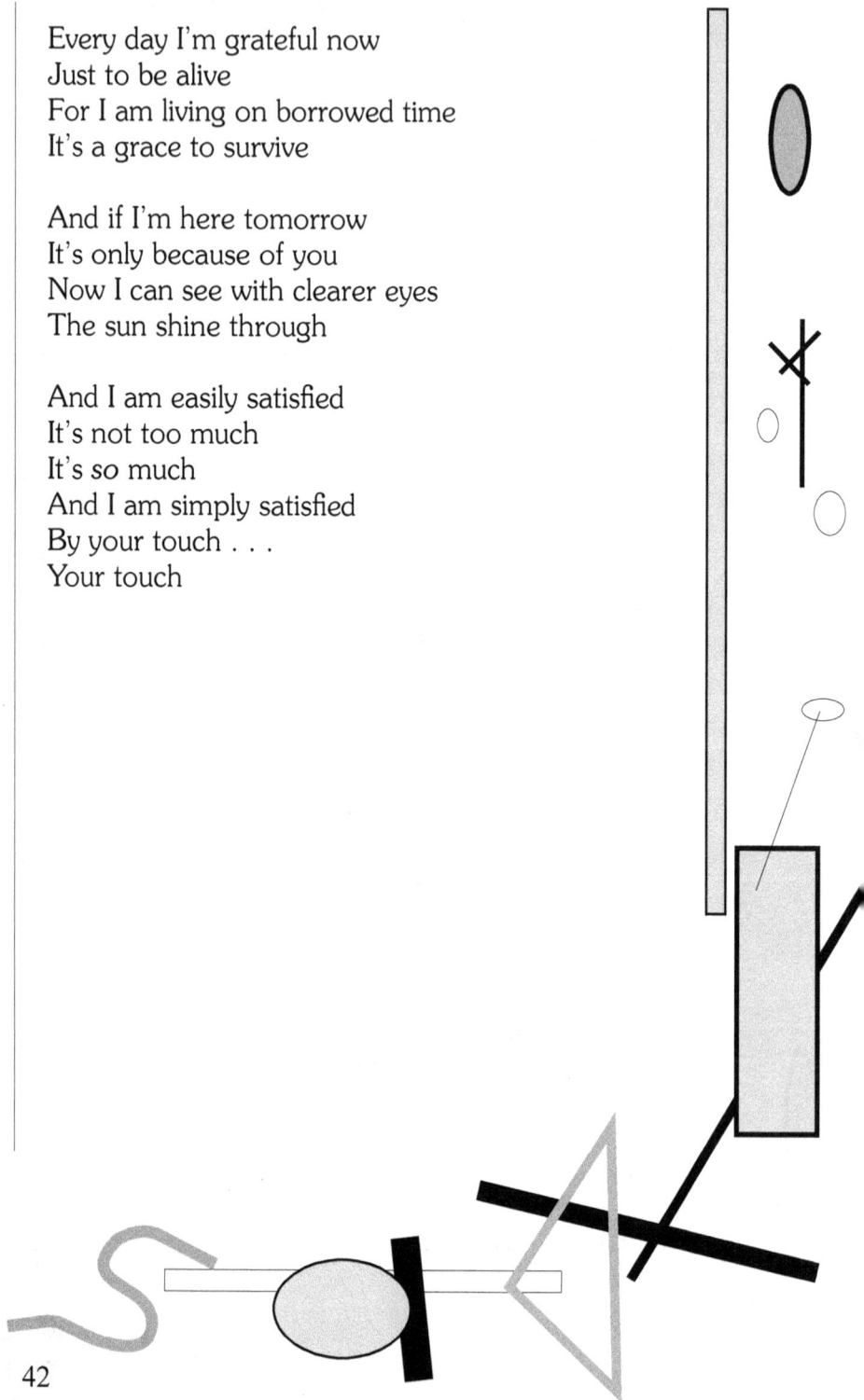

Miracle Swing

Seems like it's
A strange coincidence
What God's love
Has brought me to

Lying here
In a dream-like sequence
Half asleep
With thoughts of you

And though I feel
So restless
God's plan doesn't happen
By chance

I know that each rhyme
Has a reason
When I saw you
I knew at first glance

Take a ride
On a miracle train
Sing me a song
With a soft refrain

That shows me the joy
Life can bring
And swing me . . .
On a miracle swing

Everything in your time
        Not mine
Willingness to see
        The sun shine
Not blind, but accepting
        The patience to be
Everything
        You want for me
Loving and free
        In eternity

. . . In this moment right now

Somehow I know
        In a glance
God's plan doesn't happen
        By chance
Sometimes
        Makes me just
                Wanna dance

And yes . . . it seems like
A strange coincidence
What God's love
Has brought me to

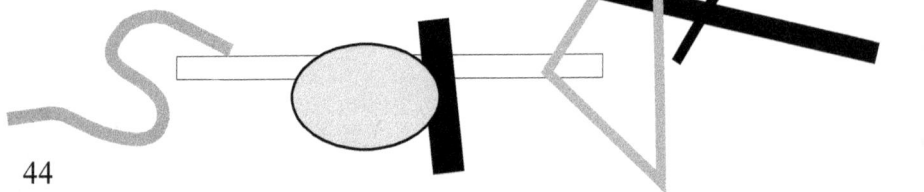

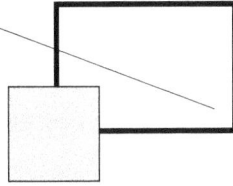

Lying here
In a dream-like sequence
Half asleep
With thoughts of you
Take a ride
On a miracle train
Sing me a song
With a soft refrain

That shows me the joy
Life can bring
And swing me . . .
On a miracle swing

And the essence
Of what I feel
Somehow doesn't quite
Come through

To the words
I'm writing right now
Or the paper
I'm putting them to

But if I can just
Express
A bit of what's in
My heart

45

If God's plan has me here
For a reason
I'm grateful
That I can take part

So take a ride
On a miracle train
Sing me a song
With a soft refrain

That shows me the joy
Life can bring
Swing me . . .
On a miracle swing

Yes . . . take a ride
On Life's miracle train
Sing me the song
With the soft refrain

That shows me the harmony
Life can bring
Swing me on . . .
The miracle swing

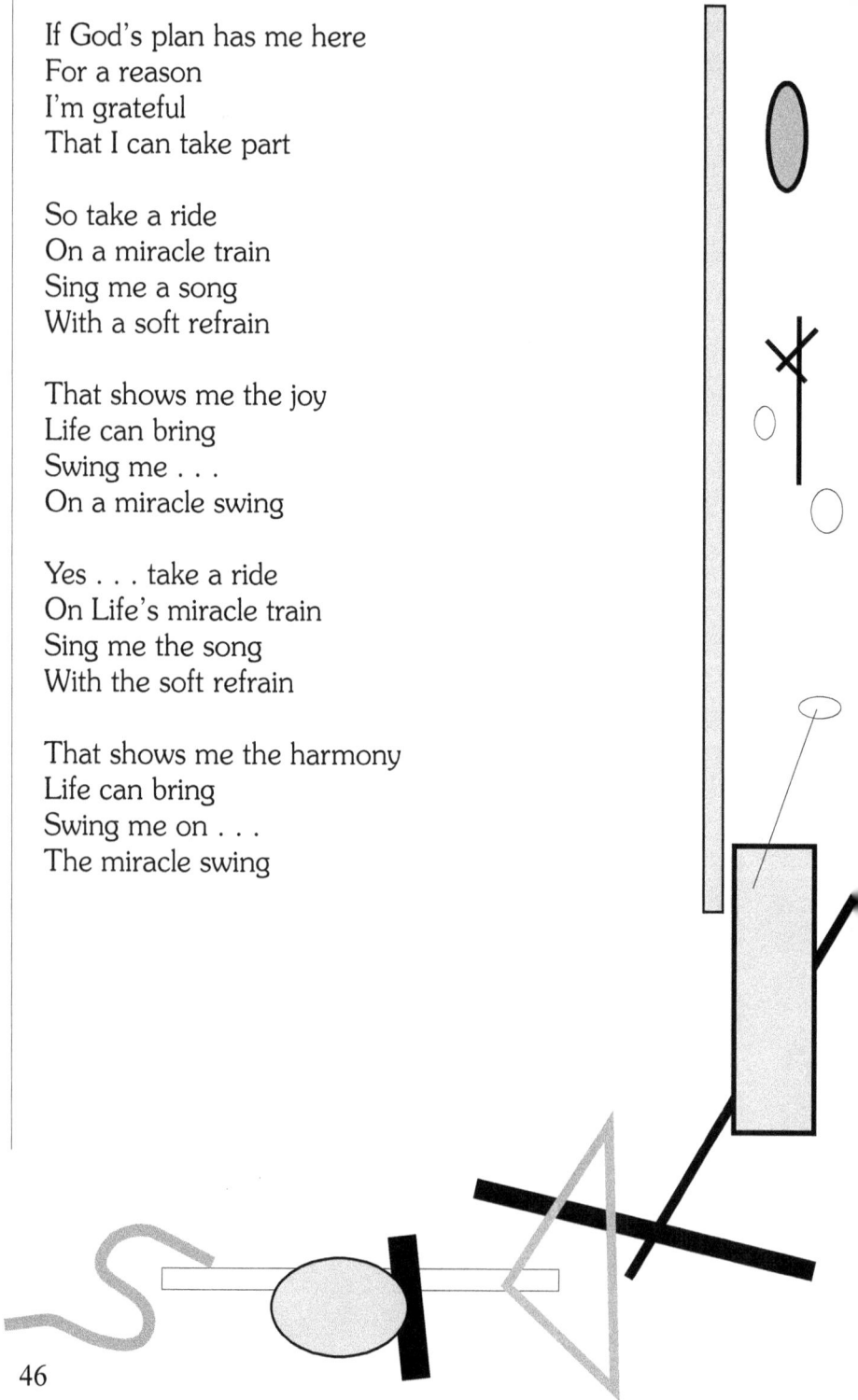

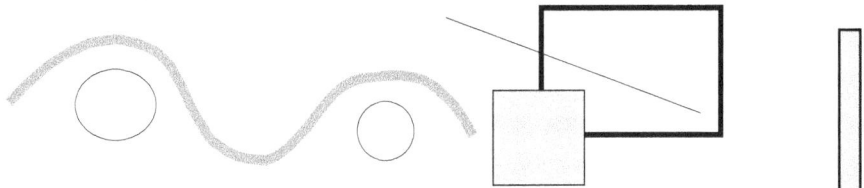

Just Yesterday

For all the glory
And the faith
And all the time
I had to wait
For all the work
We had to do
For you to get to me
And me to you

I am tired—elated
A strong appetite for kisses
But not hungry
For I feel full—fulfilled
From tip to toe

How was I to know
What you had in store

Just yesterday
I couldn't look at lovers
In the eye
Yesterday
I couldn't listen
To their sigh
Yesterday
Love songs
Made me want to cry
      Just yesterday

47

But now that you're here
I feel alive again
Feelings I'd forgotten
Grow stronger
        By the minute
                Hour and day
And yesterday feels . . .
                        So far away

Just yesterday
I knew that I would surely die
Yesterday
The tears welled up inside
Yesterday
Springtime made me sigh
And yearn to roam
Like lovers do
        Just yesterday

But today
The grass is greener
        Sky is bluer
                Love songs soar
Yesterday there was no one
But now there is so much more
        Because now . . .
        There is you

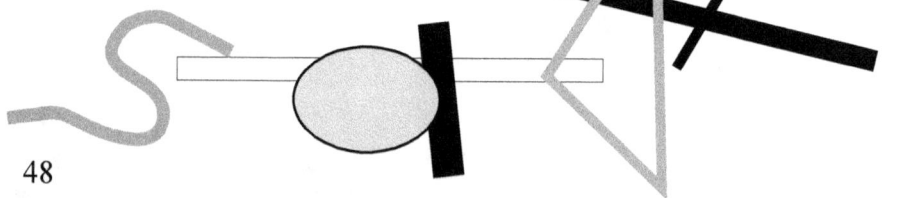

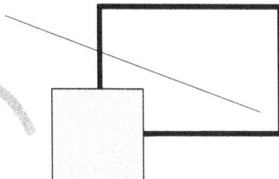

For all the glory
And the faith
And all the time
We had to wait
For all the work
We had to do
For you to get to me
And me to you

I am grateful
        You are here
                Today
And yesterday seems . . .

                        So far away

49

Arms Of The Present

I am by no means the judge
Don't wish to be the jury
I just want to lie here in your arms

I am no longer angry
Or full of fury
I am simply bedazzled by your charms

Just lying here
In the arms of the present
No longer living in the past

Trying to learn something
From each new moment
Trying to make it last

I am not longing
To touch tomorrow
I can smell the sense of today

I know that tomorrow
Will be taken care of
For this moment is leading the way

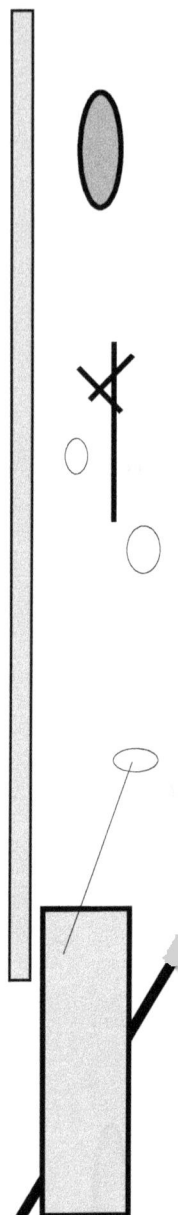

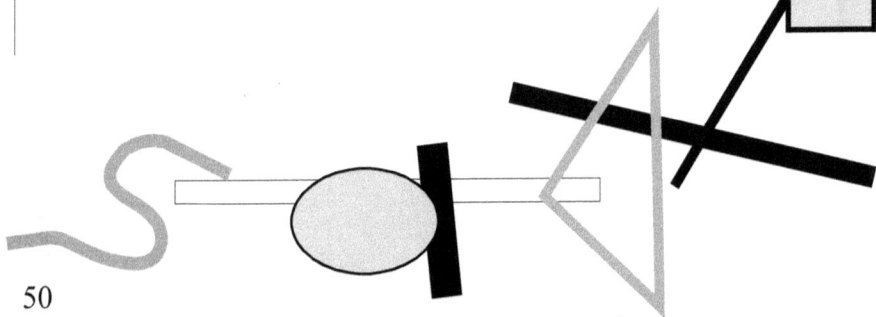

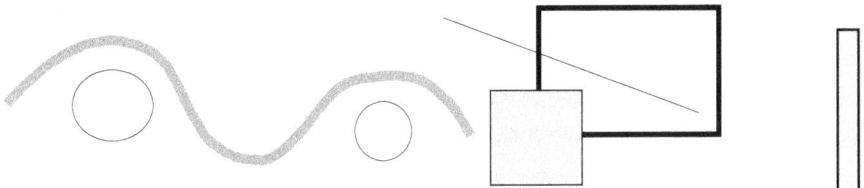

Just lying here
In the arms of the present
No longer in the past

Trying to learn something
From each new moment
Trying to make it last

Index of original composition dates

About The Author

Throughout his life, poet C. Steven Blue has experimented with music and songwriting. As a result, many of his poems are songlike. Steven has collected these poems into this series of books called *Wordsongs*; each book containing 20 poems and resembling a record album in scope and concept. We hope you have enjoyed the third *Wordsongs* album and will continue to read this unique series.

C. Steven Blue grew up in Los Angeles, California. Poetry has poured out of him since he was a boy. He won his first poetry award at age 12. However he did not start to write seriously until he was 18. That was in 1968. The tumultuous events of the 1960s were exploding all around him, inspiring him to write with greater fervor and frequency.

After various jobs in his youth, Steven began a career in Hollywood stage production that lasted 27 years. He is now retired and living in Eugene, Oregon. He continues to write and perform his own poetry, publishes his own and other's works, and produces and hosts local poetry events.

About The Symbols

PEACE BETWEEN MAN AND WOMAN

Steven designed this symbol in 1966 (at the age of 16) as a tribute to the Hippy idealism of the 1960s.

Now a registered trademark, it is both a valid and timely symbol for the third millennium.

AQUARIUS WITH LEO RISING

Steven also designed this personal symbol in 1966 as his own signature. His natal astrological sign is Aquarius, with Leo rising, represented here by the Sun (Leo's ruler) rising over the symbol of Aquarius.

About The Artwork

All of the computer graphics, symbols, pictures and illustrations in this book were created by C. Steven Blue.
All photographs are owned by C. Steven Blue.

MORE BOOKS

BY

C. STEVEN BLUE

The WORDSONGS Series:
Wordsongs (book 1)
Wordsongs—*Too Blue* (book 2)

S.O.S. ~ Songs Of Sobriety ~
A Personal Journey Of Recovery

WILDWEED

Black Tights — Poetry X

Published by

ARROWCLOUD
PRESS

For more information go to www.wordsongs.com